Love is the Answer

Swamini Krishnamrita Prana

Mata Amritanandamayi Center
San Ramon, California, United States

Love is the Answer

by Swamini Krishnamrita Prana

Published by:
 Mata Amritanandamayi Center
 P.O. Box 613
 San Ramon, CA 94583-0613 USA
 Tel: (510) 537-9417

First edition: April 2014

In India:
 www.amritapuri.org
 inform@amritapuri.org

In USA:
 www.amma.org

In Europe:
 www.amma-europe.org

Contents

THE SUBJECT TONIGHT IS LOVE.

AND FOR TOMORROW NIGHT AS WELL.

AS A MATTER OF FACT,

I KNOW OF NO BETTER TOPIC

FOR US TO DISCUSS,

UNTIL WE ALL DIE.

— HAFIZ

Chapter 1

Pure Love Embodied

"When you realise how perfect everything is, you will tilt your head back and laugh at the sky."

— *The Buddha*

Amma often tells us not to say, "I love you." Instead we should say, "I *am* love." This is a fundamental cornerstone of Her teachings, but what does it mean to actually *be* love? It is impossible to truly understand the concept of love with words, but if we allow innocence and compassion to fill our heart we will be able to experience it. If we watch Amma with humility and an open heart, we may be able to tune straight into the essence of what She is saying.

When there is pure love in our heart there is no separateness, everything simply becomes one. We are all searching for this love, but it is not so far away; rather, it is waiting patiently inside each one of us. Becoming love is what we exist for, but we tend to spend so much time looking outside of ourselves, chasing after everything else and never finding ultimate fulfilment. Instead, Amma urges us to let go of our negativities and merge into the pure love that is locked away in our heart. This is so simple in theory, but extremely difficult to do.

Amma is like a river overflowing with goodness. Her greatness lies not only in achieving the ultimate state of God-realisation, but also in going way beyond that to encompass a life of unconditional compassion. It is just a mother's nature to express love.

I remember one day in the car Amma turned to me and stroked my shoulder with such affection. It was as if She was saying, "I am just letting you know that I love you." I remember Her doing this for no reason at all; She simply overflows with sweetness sometimes – She cannot help it. Another time She called for me and started to talk about something. Then after a little while She said, "You can go now. I hadn't seen your face for a few days so I just wanted to see you." Amma desires to make everyone happy in some way or another. That is why I have never tried to demand attention from Her, because I know that whatever I really need, Amma will give.

When the catalyst of love fills our heart, it overflows in the form of compassion. On several occasions I have heard Amma say, "My path is not the path of *moksha* (liberation). My path is to love and serve the world."

This confused me the first few times I heard Her say it. I thought, 'How can I share this with anyone? They will be so disappointed since everyone thinks moksha is the goal of life.' Then I heard the second part of it.

"A *sannyasin's* (monastic) path is to forget about their own liberation. They should be ready to go down to hell to raise everybody up, forgetting themselves." I understood then that She was talking about the very highest ideal we can strive for: compassion in action.

Our goal should not be to perform spiritual practices for our own emancipation, but rather to love and serve the world because that is the highest path. Instead of praying, 'Give me liberation from this,' we should pray, 'Help me to accept the Divine will and serve the world somehow.'

Compassion is our own true nature. Unfortunately, for most people it lies deep inside, dormant and out of reach, covered over with all sorts of crud. If we want to awaken the true nature of love inside ourselves, then acquiring should not be our only goal in life; we must also learn to give. Instead of focusing on receiving, we should strive to give compassion to others whenever we can. If we want to become evolved human beings we must understand and have compassion for everyone, helping others in whichever ways we can. Compassion is Amma's philosophy. She practices love and compassion towards everyone and teaches us by Her personal day-to-day example.

People have no idea how much Amma sincerely wants to make us happy. Her goal is to remove the suffering of those in distress. Amma's each and every action is true *seva*, service for the sake of compassion.

Amma lives a life of extreme austerity, but it is austerity born of love. She always puts the needs of others before Her own. She will not eat until She has given Herself in service. While most people have at least two or three meals per day, Amma has only one, if any at all. She never eats breakfast and starts *darshan* (traditionally means 'vision' of a saint, but Amma blesses people through Her embrace) around ten or eleven in the morning. She fasts all day and through the night and only takes a meal when She returns to the room after giving darshan, often past midnight in the ashram. While travelling, Amma's programs usually finish at three or four in the morning, sometimes later. Even so, She keeps Her fast.

Amma rarely sleeps more than a few hours per night, and there are many nights when She simply does not sleep at all. She spends every waking moment focusing on how to serve, whether it is expressed through embracing people, reading the hundreds of letters She receives every day, personally managing the countless charitable projects, hospitals, orphanages and schools She has founded, or advising devotees and answering their questions. Amma has listened to literally millions of people's problems and has made Herself available to each one of them in every possible way. She has always followed a *dharmic* (righteous) path of sacrifice and service inspired by love.

That is Her life: simply to give.

Amma worships every single person who comes to Her, not the other way around. Some people have mistakenly believed that Amma wants to be worshipped, but this is far from the truth and almost laughable when one thinks about how She lives Her life. It is a sacrifice of the highest degree to be present for the public every day for hours on end, no matter how She may be feeling.

Amma is touched and grabbed by crowds of people every day and deprived of food and bathroom breaks right throughout the day and into the night. This would seem more like horrific punishment to most people. Listening to the same complaints, questions and requests over and over hundreds of times every day would surely drive us insane. Still, Amma lovingly and joyfully offers Herself to all who approach Her and has done so continuously for the last forty-five years.

Amma embodies true worship. She sees the Divine in each one of us and worships God through service, compassion and empathy. It is the power of pure authentic love that allows Her to constantly give of Herself and accomplish super-human feats.

In today's world you will not find another *Mahatma* (great soul) like Amma. There has never been anyone in history who has given more love, grace and compassion to the world than She has. She is the essence of everything Divine rolled into one. No matter how far you look, no other teacher has ever exuded as much wisdom, joy and laughter.

Amma shows the world what can be done when we have installed the Divine in our heart. She says, "You have love within; you just have to change your attitude. You are not like a light post; rather, you are like a transformer that can generate tremendous electricity. You are not like a candle that needs to be lit, but are like the self-luminous sun."

Amma reminds us constantly that we too have a Divine spark of pure love lying inside of us, waiting to ignite and transform us. We simply have to keep blowing on it and it will become like a huge bonfire, destroying our negativities and bringing light to the world.

Chapter 2

A Culture of Selflessness

"What matters is not great deeds, but great love. Holiness is an everyday thing."

– Saint Therese of Lisieux

Amma sometimes states that Her mother was Her guru. She has often told us that Her mother exemplified the traditional values of love and service. Amma has said, "I tell you that you should love others like yourself, but Damayanti Amma showed it in her actions."

When Amma was a child, the villagers would not light a matchstick or a lamp in every house. The lamp would be lit in one house and they would go around with a coconut shell and a wick, bringing the light to their own houses. Amma's mother taught Her that when She went to another house to collect fire She should always see if they needed any help. If some vessels were lying dirty, She would first clean them all, sweep the floor and help them in every possible way. Only then would She take the light, not before. Teaching Amma this way, Her mother exemplified the kind of values that ruled village life and characterised Amma's upbringing.

The source of livelihood in Amma's village was fishing, but people did not participate in an employer/employee system. Their economic structure was based instead on community support and sharing. They took care of each other, even at the expense of personal profit and gain. Cooperation was always valued over competition. The values surrounding work and money were much more community based when Amma was a child than they are today.

In the village where Her family lived most of the men were fishermen. When they returned from the sea with their catch, they sold the fish and gave away seventy-five percent of the profit, distributing it equally to all who helped. They also set aside a little for the elderly and the widows in the village who could not look after themselves. Those in need did not have to ask for anything as something was always given to them. Leftover coins were distributed to the children so they could buy sweets.

This attitude of sharing pervaded village life. Even if Amma's father did not catch anything, Her mother would still set a plate of food aside for the people next door just in case they had nothing to eat. Her family would stretch what little they had so that the nearby children would not go hungry.

It was a custom that when people visited other houses, they were always offered food. Because of this they made sure that they did not go to anyone's house until they were certain everyone in that family had eaten. They knew their host would insist on feeding them and they did not want to inconvenience anyone if there was not enough food to give. The villagers always thought about each other before themselves; it was ingrained in them to live that way. Amma says it was this essence of love that held families and communities together in those days.

On the occasion of a wedding or a festival, people quite freely offered their best clothes for others to wear. If there was a wedding in one house then all of the neighbours gave some money to help. The donations were recorded in a book, and the favours were returned at a later time. There was no hoarding because people truly lived in the present moment. The villagers did not think about saving money for the future. They never had bank accounts but lived quite simply day-to-day. This system worked because the villagers were ready to take care of each other.

When Amma was young, Her family and the village community exuded genuine love that came from the heart. Amma's childhood was full of simplicity and innocence. When the children played, everyone looked after them. People did not think as they might today, 'These are my children and my responsibility. Your children are your own responsibility.' Instead, they were all fed and looked after by all the adults in the village. Her siblings and all the village children ran together, played together, climbed in the mango trees and swam in the backwaters. Every day was like a festival celebration, as there was so much closeness between family members and villagers.

There was not much in terms of material prosperity, but the wealth of love was enormous. As a child Amma received only two sets of clothing every year, one at the Onam festival and the other at the start of the school year. She had only two sets to last a whole year.

Recently, when Amma was talking to a young boy standing at Her side during darshan, She gave him a *satsang* (spiritual talk) about poverty. She insisted that even though he was living in India, he really had no idea how most people struggle because he lives in such a luxurious way. Amma went on to say that when She was young She did not have toys; She had friends. He on the other hand has so many toys, but how many good friends does he have? On another occasion Amma saw some children playing in the sand and remarked sadly, "Children had such innocence in the olden days, but now they have playhouses instead."

Amma celebrates the mothers who give the *samskara* (culture) of selflessness to their children because in doing so, they instil good values into their families and communities. These values will help to uphold the future. Amma received this samskara in Her house, but the present generation is often missing this precious culture.

Chapter 3

Love Heals All Wounds

"In the end, nothing we do or say in this lifetime will matter as much as the way we have loved one another."

– Daphne Rose Kingman

In the early days when I sat with Amma to ask Her questions, I used to think that it was qualities such as dispassion and renunciation that we should learn from Her, but Amma kept pushing me to aim for Love. When I first came to Amma I rarely thought about love. At the time I felt that I was finally ready to start a 'real' spiritual life and wanted to aim for something higher, but Amma kept on teaching me that the power of love is the greatest force in the whole world.

With love we can do anything. In the end, love will heal all of the wounds of this world.

All truly great accomplishments have only been achieved because of an underlying foundation of love, dedication and a very good attitude. If a child is sick and has to be taken to the hospital, the parents can stay awake for days on end sitting with their child. Love can push the body past all normal limitations. It is love that gives us the strength to go on through any difficulties and obstacles that might arise in life. If we can develop true love inside of ourselves we will find that anything is possible.

There is a young child in Switzerland who has Down Syndrome. When he was very little, Amma was the only one he would call 'Mama.' He never referred to his own birth mother by this name at all. Now he is a little bit older, he can walk and often sits for meditation on the *peetham* (raised platform the Guru sits on) next to Amma. When his father turns up to take him after Amma starts darshan, I usually ask the child, "Papa or Amma?" Every time he chooses Amma over his own mother and father and runs to Her darshan chair.

At the end of darshan Amma often takes him to Her room for a little while. She carries him up the stairs even though he is incredibly heavy. I will try to help, just to take the weight off Amma, but Amma always insists, "He is not so heavy. He does not have that much weight on him."

I protest, "Amma, he is sooo heavy!"

Amma disagrees saying, "No, he is not heavy!" That is just the way Amma feels, because with love, everything becomes weightless.

One girl recently expressed the concern that her ego was so big she could barely fit in the same room with it. She was worried she would never reach God-realisation with so many faults. I told her the simple truth: no matter how big our ego or how unmanageable our mind might seem, Amma's love is even bigger and more powerful. There is no need to worry; Amma will take care of it. Her love will permeate and heal everything that needs to be healed.

When we watch Amma, we see that the power of love heals wounds of all kinds, no matter how deep they are. Love is the most powerful medicine in the world – it is like a steady I.V.

drip that we have to take over a long period of time. Though it may feel slow at times, rest assured that the power of love can surely destroy the ego. This does not mean that Amma will always heal our bodies or give us exactly what we want, but if we trust in Her grace, our heart will open up and we will find the love that lies inside. The power of a Mahatma is greater than the power of the ego.

There is a story of a devotee who was recently diagnosed with cancer. For her, Amma's grace and love have transformed this fearful process of dying into a beautiful and liberating experience, a celebration of life. I encouraged her to write about her feelings, as she has inspired many of us living at *Amritapuri* (Amma's ashram in India).

'Being diagnosed with a terminal illness has shown me that Amma's teachings, Her presence and Her patient ongoing love have given me the tools necessary to explore new realms of the one, unchanging truth. I stopped worrying about living and started to become more mindful in the present. News of the diagnosis brought Amma's teachings into a living practice within my heart, rather than an abstract thinking exercise in the mind. In my heart there is now silence and peace; for the first time, I can feel my true Self. A friend told me upon hearing my news, "It is a great gift, a blessing, to know when you will die." I certainly feel this is the truth. Thank you Amma for helping me explore my true nature.

For several years I had been feeling as though I had a big black hole of anger in my liver, so when I actually saw this on the CT scan, I really was not at all surprised. The first week I was extremely angry. I told myself that living is not all that wonderful, having been plagued with depression and anger for reasons unknown to me at several points in my life. I thought that having lots of years of experience as a hospice nurse would help my brain accept what was to be.

After this first difficult week, I surrendered to my diagnosis. I have not had any feelings of anger, depression, or fear since. This was the first sign of grace that

I noticed and for this, I am very grateful. Another devotee reminded me, "Grace is ever-present and ever-flowing. You just have to be open to it." I have surrendered deep within my heart and now accept Amma's infinite, unconditional love and all that goes with it. I find this journey exciting, exhilarating and most joyful.'

Love can solve all the problems of the world. This may not happen overnight, sometimes it takes years. Amma's love is not always a miracle cure, although it can be. Healing takes an awful lot of practical effort on our part. It can be very challenging to overturn our negativities and seek love inside ourselves.

Amma often tells the story of a small boy who saw some vomit on the floor and rushed to clean it up, when everyone else ignored it. Later that night, Her mind kept going back to him. It was such a small action that he performed. People are scrubbing away for hours every day, but does Amma think about them in Her room? Maybe, maybe not. It was this boy's selfless attitude that drew Amma's thoughts to him again and again.

One time I tried this myself. Another woman and I were at a program when a young girl suddenly vomited. We both rushed to the spot. I said, "I'm going to clean this up."

The other woman argued, saying, "No, no, I want to clean it up."

I insisted, "No, I really want to clean this up," so we argued with each other over who was going to be the selfless one to get the chance to clean it up. In the end, we cleaned it up together and felt extremely proud of ourselves. As we cleaned, we wondered where the child's mother had disappeared to. *She* should have been the one wanting to clean it up! I doubt Amma's grace flowed much at that time, but it was a funny episode.

Despite all our mistakes, Amma patiently waits for us, knowing that pure love is the answer to absolutely everything. She goes on forgiving, loving and setting a perfect example for us to follow, no matter what anyone may think or say about Her. Even when people have tried to hurt Her, Amma has always responded by forgiving and loving them in return.

Amma knows that there is a scarcity of love in this world. Love is what we are born for, but we rarely get to experience it. She wants to see people jumping in joy with love, which is why She gives so much of Her life and energy to help us experience the love we are looking for.

No words can describe the pinnacle of human existence, the state to which Amma is guiding us. It is there She dwells, living in bliss, yet She is always ready to sacrifice Herself and come down to our level to lift us higher.

Chapter 4

The Butterfly of Compassion

"Holiness is not just for a saint,
holiness is the responsibility of each
of us. We were made to be holy."

— Mother Theresa

Edward Lorenz was a meteorologist and mathematician who for many years tried to present his scientific hypothesis to other professionals. He posited that something as small as the flapping of a butterfly's wings could generate a giant hurricane on the other side of the earth.

His colleagues distrusted his simple theory, but finally after more than thirty years, it was accepted as a genuine scientific law.

The world now accepts his theory; it is commonly known as the 'Butterfly Effect.' In this same way, if we spread just a little kindness and compassion around, it could create phenomenal reactions all around the world that we might never have thought possible.

One morning, during a South Indian tour in Trivandrum, a large black and white butterfly made its way to the program. I watched from the stage as it landed on person after person, each for just a few seconds. For one man, it landed on his head, for another, on the tip of his glasses. The man wearing specs seemed to hold his breath in expectation and delight, wondering how long the butterfly would stay on him. He clearly felt the butterfly was a blessing of good luck. Every person the butterfly landed on felt the sanctification of its touch. All the people watching also felt blessed to witness the event.

A butterfly's life is short but wonderful. With its small acts of beauty, it brings so much joy wherever it goes. If a tiny butterfly can light up our lives with a simple, small flutter of its wings, just think how much more capacity we have to bring joy to the world. We do not have to accomplish great deeds to create this 'butterfly effect.' Any good thing that we do, no matter how modest it may seem, can have a phenomenal cumulative effect. In this same way, Amma's acts of kindness know no bounds. She is beyond our understanding and the ripple effects that She starts in motion travel all around the world.

Amma's love and concern extends to all of us on so many different levels. She pays practical attention to every little detail, making sure people feel happy and taken care of. When She arrives on the stage at the beginning of a program She always looks around to check that the crowd is as comfortable as possible. She directs that chairs be given if people are standing and instructs that signs be removed if they block anyone's vision. Those who need to take medicine or have special needs are brought to Her by a priority system. She is constantly catering to the needs of everyone around Her. Never before has there been a public figure who has given so much thought to taking care of others and focused so little on Her own needs.

The beautiful message that Amma quietly tries to teach us through Her thoughtfulness is that we should always think of others before ourselves. The smallest gesture from Amma can create a huge impact if we have the vision to read the subtle messages contained in Her every action.

Amma reminds us that if one tastes honey anywhere in the world, it remains true to its inherent nature. It is always sweet. Likewise, fire is always hot. In this same way, peace and compassion are universal qualities that remain the same everywhere. Everyone longs to experience their sweetness and warmth. Amma has said that if we do not pour compassion into our actions, then even the word 'love' will only remain a word in the dictionary. Without compassion we will never experience the sweetness of that feeling.

Amma's message and mission is to spread compassion. She knows that this is what the world really needs and hungers for, in order to heal. She would like to spread compassion to all people, irrespective of language, culture, nationality and religion. She knows that to repair the wounds of the past and move forward into the future, we must open our hearts to love.

There is a story of a woman who tragically lost her child and was absolutely heart-broken. At the child's funeral many people tried to console her, though they did not really know what to say. A large man quietly approached the inconsolable mother and without a single word, simply held her hand. One of his teardrops fell silently down onto her hand. His wordless sentiment, offered with heartfelt kindness and true compassion, comforted her more than anything else anyone could say or do.

Sometimes in situations with Amma, I have been with mourning family members and thought I should try to comfort them by sharing some words of wisdom about the cycle of birth and death. Instead of giving such advice, Amma just holds them tightly and says, "Shh, it's okay. Don't cry." Sometimes that is all She has been able to say to them. She holds them and comforts them and they cry in Her lap while She cries along with them. She has never said, "It just had to happen," or "It was their time to go." At these times of immense pain, Amma simply offers Her compassion. She holds those who are crying and wipes their tears, becoming one with their sorrow.

One year while we were travelling through North India on tour we made a roadside stop in a small rural village. Some of the ladies decided to go for a walk. As they walked past a small dwelling they saw a young, pretty woman looking dejected. Knowing a little Hindi, they started to talk to her.

The woman told her story: she had been married at eight years old and pregnant at thirteen. Her husband had died drunk, so now at twenty-six, she was bringing up her thirteen year-old son alone. She had no happiness in her life and the state of the other village women was the same. Married off when they were still small girls, they were miserable and had nothing in life to look forward to. Stories like this are not uncommon, especially in developing countries.

It is not only poor villagers sitting in huts who are crying. Amma also sees many affluent people dwelling in wealthy mansions who lead empty lives, filled with just as much intense pain. Everyone, everywhere, is crying out for at least a little happiness in their lives. In Her ultimate compassion, Amma has dedicated Her life to relieving such suffering all over the world.

Chapter 5

God's Love in a Human Form

"Each time you remember the truth of who you are, you bring more light into the world."

– *Anonymous*

To watch Amma is to see the expression of God's love in a tangible form. One cannot really understand Divine Power, but Divine qualities have manifested in the lives of a few very great God-realised souls throughout history. We admire and worship these Mahatmas because they embody sacred qualities such as love, compassion, detachment and forgiveness in their lives.

Amma has found the source of Divine love and She wants to share this treasure with us. Her goal is to guide us to the state of Supreme love. We can study the scriptures and read spiritual books in order to learn about the highest truth, but it is only through watching Amma that we can see this put into action.

Amma only thinks of others and never of Herself or Her own comfort. She chooses to live this way, contrary to the choices that the rest of us tend to make.

On North Indian tours, which are usually scheduled every year, we travel from the South to the Northern-most parts of India, completely by road. It is very uncomfortable on those bumpy roads and we all get thoroughly bounced around inside the vehicle. In fact, we jokingly call the camper that we travel in our 'washing machine,' because as we drive it feels like we are being tossed around inside a washer with the cycle set for heavy-duty. If you have never been inside a washing machine, you would not know what it is like, this churning around…it is definitely not set on the light cycle!

Amma's attendant is always very considerate and as soon as someone enters the vehicle she asks, "Would you like motion-sickness medicine?" She hands it out to everyone who comes with us. People always joyously climb aboard expecting something wonderful, but they never realise what they are in for.

As we climb inside I sometimes wonder, 'Who is going to be today's victim?'

People often get jealous thinking, 'Oh, travelling in a camper vehicle must be so luxurious!' But the truth is that we are stuck bumping around in a washing machine…things are never the way they seem. There is no need to be jealous of anyone.

There are two beds available to sleep on in the camper, but Amma will never use them. She always makes sure that we use them instead. She insists upon lying down on the floor with only the thinnest of bedding. All other furniture has been taken out and there is not even a chair for Amma to lean against or sit on – so She stays on the floor.

Even in Her own room at the ashram Amma always adjusts to everyone else. Amma prefers to sleep on the floor, but as She shares Her small bedroom with Her attendant and three dogs, there is no longer space. She recently started to sleep on the bed, simply to have a bit more space to stretch out. Of course, as soon as She did this one of the dogs insisted on sleeping there too.

He is not a small dog and he likes to stretch out, so he takes up almost a third of the bed. Whenever anyone tries to pull him off he growls at them and refuses to move. In order to accommodate him and keep him quiet, Amma started to sleep with Her feet and legs dangling uncomfortably off the side of the bed. After some time, She simply surrendered to his wishes, and now She sleeps with Her feet on top of the dog, which he seems quite content with. Even in Her own room, Amma barely has space to stretch Her legs. Despite all of this She surrenders to every circumstance, always making sure that everyone else is taken care of.

Sometimes I get concerned about how much She gives of Herself. Occasionally I have pleaded with Amma to stop travelling so much, giving program after program for months on end with no rest days in between. One time I asked if we could skip the North India tour, as it is so hard on Her body. She replied, "No! Those village people are so poor. They can't afford to travel down here [to Kerala]."

I suggested, "Amma, we can send buses to pick them up and bring them to the ashram." She disagreed, saying that my plan was too expensive; it would be better to travel Herself and use any extra funds to serve the needy. It is impossible to try to convince Amma to take more rest for Herself…we have tried innumerable times.

In different countries all around the world there are devotees who cry every day because they cannot be at the ashram. Amma is always thinking of them and never Her own health or comfort. Their longing and sorrow pulls Amma to constantly travel, even though life would be far easier if we just stayed home. We live in a world where most people think only of doing what is best for themselves, always asking, 'What is in it for me?' Amma lives in an entirely different way, only ever considering others first.

Amma reminds us to focus on what we can give, instead of always thinking of what we can take. Why not do good things while we can, while we still have the strength? Once our own needs have been met, it is important to be considerate and offer back what we can to the world. No one is asking so much of us. We are not expected to follow in Amma's footsteps completely. No ordinary human being really has that capacity, but if we can forget about ourselves just a little and find some time to serve, we will certainly become happier.

Whenever Amma has supervised the devotees working on the construction of houses for the poor, She has always advised them to spend their free time going out to visit villagers in their homes, to listen to people and understand their problems. She is familiar with the anguish of the disadvantaged, as they have been opening up their hearts and pouring out their troubles to Her for decades. Unlike Amma, many young people who live at the ashram and help to do the service work have not really understood the difficulties that the underprivileged have to bear; Amma knows that helping people to become aware is the first step towards fixing the problems.

There is a great deal of poverty and suffering in this world. It is our responsibility to do what we can to help those who are in pain, which is why Amma has created extensive charitable projects all around the world. She responds to those in need everywhere. Our problems and sorrows are the driving force that inspire Amma to offer Her life in service.

We should allow our heart to melt in compassion for others when we think of them, instead of always focusing on what we can acquire and take for ourselves. Amma sets such a beautiful example, offering Her maximum in every moment. Through Her example She tries to inspire just a drop of that compassion in us.

Chapter 6

Fresh as a Daisy

"May the beauty you love be what you do."

– Rumi

Amma says that the Amritapuri ashram is like a hospital. People come with a deficiency of vitamin L (love) and are in need of intensive care. Amma is the ultimate doctor: She can see right through us, deep into our souls, through all of the superficial layers of our existence. Most people see only the outside, but Amma goes deeper than anyone, seeing right through to our very core. She has an unlimited supply of vitamin L to distribute, which is exactly what She gives to whoever needs. We are so fortunate when we have the opportunity to be in Her company and watch this flow of love and empathy taking place.

Sometimes I think about how much pain Amma has in Her body from giving darshan for such extremely long hours. On some occasions She can barely bend Her neck or move Her body at all without it hurting. At times like these I wonder how She will be able to embrace five people let alone a program full of 20,000 people! Amma never thinks in this way. She knows that She has the capacity to detach Herself from the mind/body connection; She is always able to find the strength to do anything that needs to be done to serve others.

On one occasion while driving to a large interstate program, Amma was in complete agony. Every small movement hurt Her, so I could not imagine how She would be able to manage through the night with such a large crowd coming for darshan. When Amma stepped up onto the stage, She wanted to bend down and prostrate like She always does at the beginning of programs, but because of the intense pain in Her neck, that was one movement She could not do. Amma could not bend Her neck at all. As She was about to try I insisted, "No Amma!

You don't have to do that! You can just put Your hands together in *pranam* (respectful greeting)."

I felt like a bit of an idiot saying this to Her in front of everyone there (the disciple telling the Guru what to do!). It was probably all captured on film, where I am holding Amma's arm and trying to stop Her from prostrating.

Amma simply ignored me and proceeded to bow down like She always does. Nobody seeing Her do this would have known that She had any pain in Her body at all. She was just doing Her duty, forgetting about Herself and Her own health.

When Amma holds programs in the West, She keeps going late into the night, and I know that Her body must be in intense pain. When there are two programs a day, darshan may commence at ten in the morning and go until after four in the afternoon, sometimes later, depending on the crowds. By then Amma's head is sometimes spinning from lack of food and water. People watching will never really be able to understand because Amma does not want to make anyone sad by showing them how Her body actually feels.

The evening program begins about two hours later and goes late into the night, Amma often gives darshan until four or five in the morning. She sits until every single person who wants to come to Her has received Her embrace. She then has a short break in the early hours of the morning before starting darshan again at ten. Around Amma day turns into night, and night into day, as the programs merge into each other. She never thinks of the effort She is constantly making for everyone, only of the difficulties people have in waiting for so long to see Her.

When village people come to the ashram in India and the crowd is not too large, Amma often gives extremely long darshans to them. Once when Amma came back to Her room after finishing a long day, She admitted that Her body was hurting. When I asked Her why She had given such long darshans to everyone, Amma replied that the bus fares had risen a lot. She knows how much poor people sacrifice to come to Her; there are villagers who have so little that they even have to borrow decent clothes from their neighbours to visit the ashram. Amma said, "I just have to give something to them. I have to talk to them because they understand the same language, and they have sacrificed so much to come here."

Even if Amma is sick with a stomach problem or feeling nauseous, She has never cancelled a single program anywhere in the world for this reason. If She has to be sick She may go into a side room to do that, wash Her mouth out and then return to giving darshan again. No one even realises that She is suffering. At one point Amma's stomach muscles were so painfully contracted from sitting without moving for so long that She needed to wear a brace, but what did She do? She immediately gave the brace away to a poor man who came for darshan and needed one.

Late at night, or rather through the night and into the early hours of the next morning, it can be noticed how Amma sometimes goes into another level of consciousness. She lifts Her mind away from the exhausted state of Her body, laughing, giggling and completely slowing down, embracing each person longer than the previous one. She never rushes at the end of a program, never tries to finish off quickly so that

She can go and rest, like we would if we were in the same situation.

After Amma sat for fourteen hours one day during a South India tour I was expecting that She would have tremendous pain in Her body at the end of the night. When She got back to Her room, instead of resting or eating, She met with people for another hour and a half. She was offered coconut water, which She accepted but had no intention of drinking. She held the large, full glass for at least twenty minutes until I finally took it from Her, belatedly realising it must be quite heavy to hold. She had accepted the glass simply because that is what She does. She accepts everything, never wanting to reject anything or anyone.

I could only imagine how tired Her body must have been and the pain She must have had from sitting for the full day and night without moving. I would have thought that after giving darshan for so many hours, She would be experiencing fatigue and intense muscle pain, especially in Her arms. Instead, to my complete surprise, She waved Her arms around enthusiastically as She spoke. The rest of us had already started to wilt, but Amma was as fresh as a daisy. This is just the way Amma's life flows. Love sustains Her and allows Her to do the impossible.

If Amma's body were a statue, it would have rusted away and turned to dust long ago. How many people lay their hands on Amma's legs, step on Her feet, grab at Her neck or yell in Her ear? But with the grace of the Divine, Amma says She is able to continue giving darshan. Amma experiences pain in Her own body so that ours can be lessened. Such is the unfathomable love that a *Satguru* (true teacher) has for the world. This principle is what Christians believe when they say that Jesus suffered for our sins.

A devotee once asked Amma if Her body really suffers or not. They felt that it surely must with all that Amma has to go through, but this person was confused as Amma usually looks so happy. Amma replied, "On the human level, the body suffers, but on my level, Never! You don't worry, my dear."

A gift once given should never be taken back – She insists, "I gave myself as an offering to the world; I am not going to take anything back to think about myself." Amma shows us the way. She teaches us how to sacrifice for others by the example She sets in Her own life. She always strives so hard to give the maximum in everything that She does. When we have love in our heart, our striving to do something good becomes effortless and empowering. Let us all pray that we might be able to absorb something good from Her, no matter how small it may be, to give back to society.

Chapter 7

The Highest Sadhana

"Right from the moment of our birth, we are under the care and kindness of our parents, and then later on in our life when we are oppressed by sickness and become old, we are again dependent on the kindness of others. Since at the beginning and end of our lives we are so dependent on others' kindness, how can it be in the middle that we would neglect kindness towards others?"

– Tenzin Gyatso, 14th Dalai Lama

To love and serve others is the highest *sadhana* (spiritual practice) that we can ever perform, but how many of us are really ready to love everyone and serve all the time like Amma does? If we were truly able to love and serve unconditionally, then we would not need to do anything else to reach spiritual heights, but that includes loving

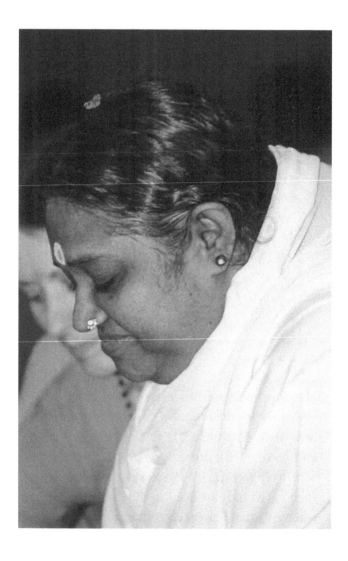

everyone, not just the few people that we might feel comfortable with or attracted towards.

It means loving the person who is cutting in front of you in the food line or someone who half sits on your lap in the *bhajan* (devotional song) hall when you already feel that you do not have quite enough space, the one who almost knocks you over or stands in front of you just when Amma is coming. If you can love them in that moment, then you do not have to do so many other kinds of sadhana.

It is extremely difficult to see the best in everyone all the time. This is the highest attitude that we can have, but it is very challenging to achieve. To begin moving in this direction, we should train our mind to concentrate on doing good things. Meditation, puja, devotional singing, mantra japa, prayers for the well-being of the world and *karma yoga* (selfless actions) are all different ways to develop concentration, compassion and empathy.

Today there are all sorts of different studies and research being conducted in the area of neuroscience that prove how good actions or even just good intentions have an extremely beneficial effect on our health and well-being. Tests have proven that the mind can be re-trained to learn positive values, even if we did not learn them as children. When we start to practice positive values, we begin to experience profound feelings of joy and wellness. A cycle is created where the more we want to do good for others, the happier we become, and the happier we are, the more we desire to perform good actions.

The impact that Amma has on children is especially beautiful as children are deeply influenced by the atmosphere that they are surrounded by. A sweet example happened with some of the children around Amma. They asked each other how many ice creams they needed to eat each week and decided that two really was enough. They happily used the money they saved from not buying extra ice cream to buy something for disadvantaged children instead. Just being around Amma inspires us to give, which is the real goal of all spiritual practices.

Sometimes the ashram children come up to me and say, "Look how many mantras I did!" One young child recently did just that and said, "Look!" as he pushed his digital mantra counter up under my nose. The number showing on it was 8,888. I was very impressed.

I asked him, "Did you say your mantra with every single number?"

"Yes!" came the little six year-old's innocent reply.

The devotion that children learn from Amma is a beautiful thing and very important in today's world. Devotion leads towards the desire to love and serve society and Mother Nature right from a young, impressionable age. This attitude of service must be nurtured for future generations to survive.

Some people may feel that they do not have time to work for others because their schedule is full of work and family. How can they possibly squeeze in service if they do not have time to spare? Amma gives the example that if you have three children, simply think of doing something to serve others selflessly as your fourth child. You would be able to take care of all of your children no matter how many there were. Like this, we should also find a little time to squeeze selfless service into our busy schedule.

We may think that our seva does not really matter, that it is not so important or that there are other people to do it, but in reality it is our most valuable tool. Seva will take us beyond thinking only about ourselves and what we want. This action, when coupled with the correct attitude and Amma's grace, can lead us to the final goal.

A man once indignantly told me how unhappy he was with his seva, "I came to Amma's ashram in order to advance spiritually for the good of humanity, and I am being asked to do menial tasks such as dishwashing and recycling. I'm a professional and very creative. I feel offended to be asked to adjust my sadhana schedule and do tasks that I just don't like."

I told him that if he was so professional at doing what he did out in the world, then maybe it was the Divine plan for him to learn a little humility by doing these other tasks. Everything in life comes to us exactly as we need. There is no mistake in the way the cycle of life presents itself to us, even if it is in the form of the seva desk coming to haunt you, asking you to serve while you would rather be doing other types of sadhana (or something much more fun).

When we sit down to meditate, even the thoughts that come up in our mind are forms of action – when we are meditating, we are still performing action. Why not also try to do some selfless service along with that, which will bring us the blessing of grace.

When the need arises, we can try to adjust our attitude to be ready and happy to do anything to help others. Amma does not need people sitting next to Her, handing Her the face towel, like I do. That job is already taken, but all sorts of other things need to be done. If they are not done, then Amma will often be the first one to come along and do what is required. She is always working hard, giving selflessly and trying to inspire us to do the same.

One evening after bhajans Amma was telling me how much pain She was experiencing. She kept saying how She wasn't feeling well at all. I felt so sad for Her, but there was nothing I could do to help, so after our conversation I went downstairs to my room to do seva. Suddenly I heard everybody rushing around and calling out, "Brick seva!"

I thought to myself, 'Well, Amma certainly won't be coming; She isn't well.' The next thing I knew Amma was outside, happily carrying bricks (more bricks than anybody else, in fact!). Sometimes She is like a child who can be distracted and easily re-directed to Her favourite activity: service.

There is a little four year-old boy in Canada who loves to do seva. One day he was wearing his adult-sized apron (which was trailing on the ground) when Amma walked past. He offered his pranams to Her and Amma turned to him saying, "Seva, seva, seva!" She was so happy to see that he had been doing seva (and he looked so cute in his enormous apron) that She gave him a kiss.

Amma often talks about the children who love to serve. She is proud and always extremely happy when She sees them working hard with the right attitude, doing something practical to help others. Seva also allows children to learn life skills for the future while developing love and compassion in their hearts. When we find

the joy in doing good things we will truly find happiness inside. Seva is one of the greatest gifts.

Spirituality is total practicality. When Amma perceives a need somewhere, She is always ready to fulfil it. That is what it is really all about: seeing what is needed and diving in to help with a loving heart. We are so lucky when we have the opportunity to serve, but it is up to us to see this as a blessing. If you find yourself thinking, 'I don't want to do this,' then somehow you have got to persuade your mind to change its attitude. If you can, you will be able to enjoy absolutely everything. No one can force you to enjoy serving others; it has to dawn from inside your own heart.

Countless seekers have read books about spirituality and different schools of philosophy, but how few are ready to do what needs to be done? How many people are really prepared for the most extreme types of humility and service? In truth, not so many at all – but what can be greater than that?

Wherever you are in the world, if you have the innocent attitude of dedicating whatever you are doing to the Divine and serving however you can, then grace will definitely flow towards you. The magnificent vehicle of service is one of the greatest joys that I have found in my life. Love is the whole point of life and selfless service is the beautiful channel through which love flows.

Chapter 8

The Secret to Happiness

*"As you help those in need, selfishness will
fall away, and without even noticing
you will find your own fulfilment."*

– Amma

When we give, we always feel extraordinarily good about ourselves. Volunteers for charitable organisations and donors to any kind of philanthropic association know the joys of an expansive mindset. It is said that money cannot buy happiness, but it is a proven fact that if you strive to give generously, you can indeed catch hold of that elusive happiness everyone is searching for. When we are able to forget our own desires and reach out to help others, this brings a very high degree of life satisfaction. In essence, the more people give, the happier they become.

One young lady was at a big family gathering, telling everyone she had the most beautiful heart. All gathered around admiring her perfect, round, smooth, glowing heart. She was so proud, boasting about this.

Suddenly an old lady's strong, rough voice called out that her heart was much more beautiful. All the guests laughed when they saw the old woman's heart. It was battered, full of patches and open wounds. Places were cut out and other places had odd sized pieces fit in. The young lady laughed and said, "How can you compare your old, distorted and torn heart with my perfect one?"

The old woman replied, "I agree that your heart is perfect but it is not beautiful. Every scar you see in my heart represents someone I have given my heart to. Sometimes they gave me a piece of theirs, but not always. That is why there are so many places where the pieces do not quite fit. But I cherish them as they remind me of the love and beautiful memories that we shared. These open wounds are painful because some people never gave their heart back, but I wait, hoping that one day they will understand the value of giving love."

The young girl cried and walked towards the old woman. She cut a piece out of her perfect heart and filled a gap in the old lady's heart. She looked down at her own heart, not so 'perfect' anymore, but much more 'beautiful.'

We occasionally come across heroic spirits who deeply inspire us. The teacher of a fourteen year-old boy was moved by the plight of one of her students, a boy dying for want of a kidney transplant. This woman told the boy's family that she would give him one of her kidneys if she proved to be a match for him. She was, and she did.

During Christmas in Philadelphia a few years back, a couple entered a restaurant, enjoyed their breakfast and then did a very unusual thing. They paid double the amount necessary for their own meal and insisted on paying the bill of the customers at the table next to them, although they were complete strangers. They did not want any praise or recognition, so they did not leave their names. They just wanted to do something nice. They told the waitress simply to wish the people a 'Merry Christmas.'

The good deed did not stop there. The customers who received this kind gesture were inspired to pay it forward. They paid for others' meals and also left tips for all of the waitresses. Each recipient was amazed to receive a free meal and insisted on passing the blessing onwards. It travelled for hours, on and on around the restaurant like a domino effect.

The waitresses who worked in the restaurant that day had never seen anything like this in all the years they had worked there. Tears formed in their eyes as they contemplated the wonderful chain reaction of generosity they witnessed over the next five hours. Like a ripple in a pond that travels out further and further, so too is the domino effect we can create when we set a selfless example and do kind things for others.

Loneliness comes when we think only of ourselves. If we are too firmly attached to what we want, then we will always feel empty – even if our pockets are full. A house filled with countless treasures cannot satisfy the heart. Our possessions may increase; our bank account may overflow, but when we blindly follow selfish desires, our mind only fills with more desires. We can get anything that we want from the world, but if we merely follow our selfishness, happiness will elude us. We will always feel that we are lacking something. Until we learn to give, our desires will never go away.

People often ask themselves, 'What am I going to get in this life?' But this is not the attitude Amma is encouraging. Instead, She inspires us to create something magnificent by finding our talents and using them to serve. Helping others brings the ultimate joy and fulfils the meaning and purpose of our lives. It is what life is for.

Desires pull us away from true happiness. When we fulfil our desires, this does not make them go away. Instead, they multiply and will surely come again. Take for example so many people's obsession with the latest technology. We get a new, updated phone and are so happy with it, but six months later the next model comes out. It is slimmer, lighter, has more pixels, more apps, more games…and we covet that one instead. We think, 'This old phone is no longer bringing me the joy it did when I first bought it. I know I will be happier with a new one!' The problem is that we cannot bring fulfilment to the mind, and the thoughts and desires that come up will never cease.

If we can simplify our desires, we will be happy even if we have less. It is good to pray for help in overcoming our desires. This is difficult to do because the mind is always moving, but that is why we chant our mantra and live a balanced life with meditation and other spiritual practices. When we stick to a spiritual discipline our desires will decrease and we will find peace.

There are so many takers in the world, but it is far better to give – only then will we find real joy. Grace comes from performing good actions with a selfless attitude. If we try to do something good with a selfless attitude behind it, then we will experience Divine grace no matter where we are in the world.

Forget yourself in selfless service. When we do not focus on our own emancipation but instead dedicate ourselves to serving others, Divine grace will come and wash over us like a river. We will receive the life-changing reward of purification and the ultimate grace will come to take us to the goal.

Chapter 9

Love Amma in Everyone

"God plus mind is man. Man minus mind is God."

– Anonymous

When people get married they tell each other, "I love you, I love you. I promise to stay with you until death do us part." Then, when things get tough, they forget about their vows. This is how deep our love is these days. However, when love becomes the firmly rooted foundation of our lives, it will produce delightfully scented blossoms – we will become like flowering jasmine plants offering exquisite fragrance to the world. Everyone we encounter can enjoy the beauty of this flower of love.

Wherever we go everybody tries to touch Amma's hand as they call out, "I love you, I love you, I love you Amma." If you really love Amma, do not just say so, put that love into practice. Love should be a verb, not just a word that we overuse without thinking. When you turn your love into actions, you will find the lasting experience and transformative power inherent within it. Without action, 'love' is like a wax fruit that looks pretty but cannot nourish us – it is just an empty, decorative shell of a word.

When we do something with love, we will be taken higher and higher out of suffering to a more peaceful place where grace unfolds. Rather than looking and seeing only one dimension of Amma, Her genuine essence will be revealed and the magnificence of love will be unveiled.

A devotee tells a story, "One time when I went for darshan I had an immense longing in my heart to be close to Amma. I asked Her in a note, 'Amma, how can I be closer to You?' Amma gazed deeply into my eyes. She stared at me and held me for a long time. When I sat down after receiving darshan, I closed my eyes and all I saw was Amma everywhere. I saw Amma in a mother loving her child, in the person helping a beggar, in friends giving love and support in times of need. Wherever there is love, that is where Amma is. I didn't want to open my eyes because I was afraid if I did I would be distracted by Her form. I realised that She is so much bigger than Her body. The experience seemed to last forever… She showed me where She was in each of my darkest moments, revealing to me that She has been supporting and holding me throughout my entire life. I was shown that Amma is love everywhere, in everything. I now know that anytime I experience love from anyone – that is Amma loving me. Amma is love in its purest form. If I want to feel Amma, all I have to do is to become that love as well. I want to become an act of love."

Amma does not need anything from us, but She would be so happy if we could truly put Her teachings into practice. We always want to make Her happy, but how can we do it? We have to do something that would be important: we have to love other people as we love Amma.

It is so easy to love Amma. It is not difficult to do at all because She is so irresistible. To devotees She is the most beautiful being on this earth, the most enchanting, the most fun, the most service-minded in every area. Amma wins first prize always. I am not surprised when people say they love Her so much because Amma is so absolutely great. Anyone with even a small amount of common sense can recognise Her greatness. Instead of only loving Amma's form, we should try to carry our love into the practice of seeing and loving everyone as Amma. Now that would really be something great (and something much more challenging)!

In the Bible Jesus says, "Love one another as I have loved you." The essence of all religions is saying exactly the same thing: God is Love. It is our duty to strive to become love as well. Amma wants us to love one another as She loves us.

Amma's practical way of moving in the world is the ultimate living example for us. Throughout everything that She has to deal with, throughout all the major problems that arise when serving millions of people, She is still able to love everyone. This is because She sees Herself in all of us and knows the truth, that this world is simply a Divine manifestation. She sees everyone as Her own reflection in the mirror. While we may believe this to be true and understand it intellectually, Amma actually, quite literally *lives* the experience of it.

She often reminds us, "According to Indian philosophy there is no difference between creation and the creator; they are one and the same, just as there is no difference between gold and golden ornaments." Amma declares that Vedanta is the Supreme Truth: everything is God. This is the ultimate understanding. But it is mainly through *bhakti* (devotion) that we can become better people by developing good qualities such as compassion and the desire to serve those in need. When we truly love God, we will have compassion for the whole world. The vibrations that are created through selfless actions born of love bless the environment and all those around. This explains why there is a tangible vibration that we can feel around great spiritual Masters, if we are perceptive enough.

A few years ago, a reporter was curious about what Amma did in Her free time so he asked Her, "What do you do when you're alone?" Everyone laughed for we knew the answer already: Amma is never alone! She is always surrounded by people, even in Her room. There are endless project meetings, someone visiting, or at least Her attendant is always with Her. Amma has no private life...She is never alone.

To our surprise, Amma clearly and simply replied, "I'm always alone."

"I don't believe you!" He answered. "I mean, what do you do when there aren't all these people around you?"

She repeated, "I'm always alone. If many people are there, or if nobody is there, I'm alone. I see all as extensions of myself; it's all one consciousness."

He still did not understand, so he offered some alternatives: "When you're alone, do you read books, or surf the internet?" There was more laughter from those who know Amma well. Amma on the web? Can you picture it? Of course not.

She responded calmly, "The external internet is a manifestation of the internal internet.

I have the Supreme internet inside, so I browse that." Amma sees everything as a manifestation of God, of Her Supreme Self. There is nothing separate from Her.

We should try to see the world like Amma does. In the early days I never went for darshan much but when watching others receive darshan I often imagined myself as the one in Amma's arms and I felt happy. If we can overcome jealousy and *feel* like we are that other person receiving love from Amma, and be happy for them, then our lives will be deeply enriched. We should share that feeling of everyone being connected somehow. In truth, we *are* everyone else...

Amma shares Her life, wisdom and infinite compassion with whoever wishes to partake. She totally merges into us when She touches us, laughs with us or sings to us. She sees everyone as an extension of Her Self. Amma is not just an ordinary human being, She is an incarnation of love in the highest degree.

Chapter 10

Detachment is Love in Disguise

"The entire world and the things in it are for our use - not for our possession. We have forgotten how to use the world and instead expect happiness from it."

– Amma

Pure joy arises from selfless giving, and peace of mind comes from serving others without expectation of reward. Ideally we want to move through life loving everyone but remaining a little detached. If we try to find happiness from the outside world, where we often tend to look for it, we will be disappointed, finding frustration and sorrow instead. Lasting happiness can only be achieved through compassion and detachment.

Most people misunderstand the real meaning of detachment. It does not mean shunning objects or abstaining from their use. It does not mean negating love and closeness in relationships (and it certainly does not mean abstaining from chocolate!). True detachment is a deep and full sense of compassion. It is the foundation of genuine love, it is selflessness and it means fully understanding the fundamental nature of an object or relationship – detachment means realising that people and objects cannot give us lasting happiness.

When we are attached to someone or something, we expect to achieve happiness through that person or object. This misconception leads to expectations and desires. Eventually, all attachment leads us towards some kind of sorrow (especially if we eat too much chocolate!). When we want something from someone else, we are experiencing attachment, not love. What we often call 'love' is really a form of bargaining, 'You give me what I want, and I will give what you want.' True detachment allows us to love unconditionally and serve without desiring anything in return. To genuinely love others is an exceptionally tall order to follow.

When the ashram residents went to build homes for the poor, especially after the 2006 Indian Tsunami, they often experienced difficulties like verbal abuse and harassment from some of the people they were trying to help. When they returned to the ashram to tell Amma of their difficulties they complained, "Amma, why should we help such people? They won't lift a finger to help with even the smallest task. They don't appreciate our work at all!" Amma explained to them that these people were simply showing their nature. In response, the ashram residents, as spiritual seekers, should show their nature as well. They should exemplify the good values that Amma taught them.

There is a traditional story about a man who keeps trying to save a scorpion from drowning. Every time he reaches his hand into the water to save it, he gets stung. Someone asks him why he keeps trying to save the creature that is repeatedly hurting him. He responds that it is the scorpion's nature to sting, but it is his nature to keep on trying to help, no matter what. He knows that helping others is the pathway to heaven.

If we expect appreciation for all of the good things that we do, we will constantly be disappointed. Instead, we must find satisfaction in the simple act of doing the right thing. With enthusiasm and the correct attitude any action we perform can be a beautiful experience. Even if no one ever gets to see it or know about it, we will reap enjoyment from doing something good.

Clinging to people and wanting them to like us is a form of attachment that will eventually bring disappointment. Amma shows us through Her own life how to have compassion for everyone, even those who are cruel to us. She offers only love and forgiveness, even to those who have publicly lied about Her or tried to kill Her. She teaches us how to love everyone, regardless of how they feel about us. Having that much detachment is not an easy feat.

Loving everyone does not mean blindly trusting everyone, we still must use our discrimination. A young man came to me and related an incident that happened to him one night in Mumbai. He was a little unsure if he had done the right thing or not. A thief approached him on the street, put a knife to his throat and demanded he hand over all of his money. Instead of doing what the thief said, he grabbed the knife, punched him in the face (breaking his nose) and ran for his life, keeping the knife as a souvenir. I assured him that in this case, he had done exactly the right thing.

Sometimes it is important to fight back for a just cause. Obstacles will most definitely arise in life. We must maintain the correct mental attitude and learn to properly flow around them. In this case, the man had not been angry with the thief who tried to rob him; in fact, defending himself had been the most compassionate action he could have chosen. Perhaps it inspired the thief to think deeply about whether or not he should continue with his bad career choice.

We should try to understand the basic nature of people. When we remember that all people have flaws, it becomes easier to forgive and have compassion for others, instead of blaming or judging them for their limitations. If we can maintain this understanding, it will help us to be empathetic towards everyone and will eventually lead us to a final state of selfless love.

People who come to Amma's ashram sometimes think that because it is a holy place everyone will be quiet and gentle, always immersed in their spiritual practices. That may seem true until you get into the chai line for a cup of tea. There you may see some less than saintly behaviour. When our desires are blocked, anger from the ego arises. We have to understand that this is the nature of the ego and the nature of the world. Our grumpy faces arise when desires come charging forward.

As Amma says, "We should not try to turn a frog into an elephant or an elephant into a frog. Try to see others for who they are, not who we want them to be. When we go to a zoo there will be wild animals, lions and tigers. We do not go close to those animals, instead we stay far away and enjoy. If we go too close it is dangerous. Like this, we should always leave a gap inside, separating ourselves from what is happening and trying to become a witness to it. In this way we will be able to remain calm and peaceful inside, despite all external circumstances."

If we can maintain internal detachment, we will be able to enjoy the world without getting adversely affected by all the ups and downs of it. There will always be people we love who are incredibly kind to us, and others we dislike because they are difficult to deal with. We will find it easier to empathise with those we do not like if we look into their history, trying to understand their problems, pain and suffering. This process will draw forth our inherent compassion and help it to grow. When we get to know the people who upset us, we will very often see that they came from extremely sad or challenging backgrounds.

Most of the time we are not conscious of how deeply other people are suffering and we misjudge them. Perhaps those who are difficult were abused or did not receive enough love from their parents. Amma says that even in the womb, a baby may not form properly if there were not loving intentions behind its creation. Perhaps the person came from parents who were alcoholics or drug addicts – these children often carry lasting wounds throughout their lives. If we can understand situations with a broader perspective, we can free ourselves from the chains of bondage that come from our judgmental ways of thinking.

Amma tells us, "Don't be like a camera. Be like a mirror." Reflect, release, and be detached. Amma never gets caught up in negative emotions; She is a pure reflection, witnessing with love and mirroring ourselves back to us. She does not hold onto anything but lets everything pass through Her without judgment. We, on the other hand, are more like cameras taking photos of every single scene to use as evidence. The incredible freedom that stems from detachment allows Amma to do what nobody else can: love each one of us unconditionally and embrace thousands of people, one after the other.

While moving in the world, we must learn to understand others properly and love everyone without any expectation of reward. Amma is asking us to understand people's situations, their circumstances, their mental constitutions, and then serve them.

Chapter 11

Creating Internal Freedom

*"Hatred never ceases by hatred,
but by love alone is healed."*

— *Buddhist verse*

If we cannot let go of the negative experiences that happened to us in the past, we will never be able to grow. It is only through forgiveness that we can heal our pain. People hurt us mainly because they are suffering themselves. When we develop a compassionate vision to see beyond the outer façade, we will notice the far-reaching effects of pain in countless lives. This cycle of pain will continue until we untangle ourselves from the bondage of our mental concepts and learn to forgive. It takes a very great person to forgive, especially when someone else is at fault.

Divine retribution will definitely come to those who have hurt us. We should have nothing to do with purposely aiming to deliver it. It is detrimental to desire vengeance or punish people for the ways they have hurt us. Everyone revolves in their own karmic cycle. All the pain that we inflict on others will return to us one day – so why hurt ourselves in the future by seeking revenge? Instead, let us simply learn from our own difficult experiences. Who knows what we did in other births to bring suffering upon ourselves?

Amma gives the example, if we are walking in the dark and trip over a thorn bush or a barbed wire fence, we will get hurt by it. Instead of letting it go and concentrating on healing the pain, we keep on clinging to the barbs, shouting, 'You hurt me, let me go, let me go!' In fact, we are the ones holding on. Even though it is only for our own good, we are not yet ready to release our grip on the pain we are causing ourselves. One day we will have to let it all go. Why not do it sooner, rather than later, after we have become scarred from so much self-inflicted agony and trauma? Why not forgive and be free?

It is for our own benefit that we learn to forgive. As for the pain that we have had to experience, we may never really understand why it had to come. There are some things in life that we will never be able to understand, some things we cannot even try to fathom. To heal ourselves, we must accept that this pain was our *karma* (the law of cause and effect) coming back to us and forgive those who were the Divine vehicles sent to deliver the message.

One afternoon at the beach in Amritapuri, Amma gave a satsang about the coming New Year. She said that instead of making resolutions, we should make an effort to forgive. If we have gotten into fights or stopped talking to someone, we should be the ones to apologise and seek forgiveness. She has given this satsang on a number of occasions, telling us that if we have estranged family members, we should be the ones to reach out and forgive. During this particular occasion, one devotee reluctantly realised what he had to do.

While sitting at the satsang he sent an email on his phone to his stepfather and apologised for the bad relationship that they had. He asked for forgiveness and said that even though they had not gotten along for twenty years, he would like to start over. His stepfather was extremely touched and overwhelmed with joy. He immediately agreed to a fresh start. When this devotee went back to visit his mother and stepfather a few months later, he found out that his stepfather had been diagnosed with terminal cancer and only had a few more months to live.

The relationship that blossomed from their reconciliation led to the devotee becoming his stepfather's caretaker for the last few months of his life. In the end, this devotee was the one who sat by his stepfather's bed and held his hand as he transitioned into death. Their healing time together forged a precious relationship, which became an amazing spiritual journey for them both.

We must learn to pray for those who hurt us. Pray that we are able to forgive them and that they are able to bear the pain and suffering they will have to experience due to their actions. Let go of the 'thorn bush' and embrace forgiveness. If you can do this, then life will surely embrace you back ever so sweetly.

Another devotee shared her experience from following Amma's satsang advice.

She said, "My youngest brother worked in the World Trade Centre for many years. He was in the building on the day of the attacks. After the first plane hit his building he was able to escape with a number of his co-workers; they were preparing to go into the second tower when the second plane hit. They ran and escaped again.

Communication was down so we did not know all day if he had survived. After the attacks my brother would never speak of his pain and trauma. He never sought counseling, he wouldn't talk to either his wife or me about it; he just tried to pretend it didn't happen. I knew he was suffering but I didn't know what to do to help him.

Amma teaches us to love our family members when they are suffering, but at that point my brother and I had not had regular contact for fifteen years. Many family problems existed and this led to a deep distance between us. I heard Amma's satsang that we should write to estranged family members, to pray for them and to gently communicate our love for them. She said even if you don't know what to say, just email or write them a short letter expressing your loving concern. She made us say out loud in the hall that we would write to our family members. So I committed to writing. This began twelve years of writing to my brother.

On September 11th every year I would text him a short note. I would express my love and understanding about his suffering, as well as my gratitude that he was alive. I told him that I am always here for him if he wants to talk.

Year after year passed but he never responded. Amma teaches us to love without expectation – and so every year I would send the message and continue to pray. A few years ago, on September 11th, I felt my phone vibrate. I looked down and for the first time in years there

was a text from my brother. He had for-
warded me all of the text messages I had
sent from the previous decade with a
note that said, 'I saved your text messages
every year and I read them throughout
the year. You have no idea how much
they've meant to me all of this time.'

I scrolled through and read messages
I had written to him once a year – for
years and years – never knowing if he read
them, whether he liked them or whether
they brought him comfort. I began to cry.
Amma showed me that love and reconciliation is even more powerful than the
pain of terrorism. Like drops of water on
a rock, eventually love will win."

We have a choice in life: either we can fall into
more suffering or we can climb towards forgiveness and internal peace. One must be incredibly brave and humble to walk on the road of
forgiveness – most people are not quite ready
for that heroic venture. A spiritual seeker must
remember that it is only through forgiveness that
we can rise higher, difficult though it may be. If
you hold on to the past, it is not going to help

you at all. If you want to move forward towards God, you must learn to forgive and forget.

When people throw manure, what does a plant do? It absorbs the minerals from that smelly fertiliser and uses them to grow. It does not think, 'Oh, what have you done to me?' The flowers flourish, absorbing only the nutrients from the muck and using them to blossom into beautiful flowers. Just like this, with forgiveness we can become like magnificent spiritual flowers exuding the rare perfume of selfless love.

Chapter 12

Forever a Beginner

"To escape criticism - do nothing,
say nothing, be nothing."

— Elbert Hubbard

When we first come to Amma, we may think that we are pretty close to perfect and closing in on the threshold of Self-realisation. But after some time, as the years pass by and others inevitably trigger our hidden negativities, we begin to discover that we might not be quite as perfect as we initially thought. Similarly, we may think the kitchen floor is clean, but when we start to wipe it with a wet cloth, all kinds of filth comes up. When we are honest with ourselves we start to notice just how far we really are from perfection – we are right back at the starting line, forever a beginner.

Noticing our flaws is a very good starting point on the road towards humility. When the illusion of our niceness is shattered we can start to pick up the pieces, becoming more honest with ourselves. Spiritual practices are like a wet cloth that cleans away the impurities from our mind. They help us to become more aware, to clean up our act and make ourselves whole.

If we make a mistake, we should not just stop; we have to go on and learn how to correct it. If we fall down, we should not simply lie on the ground and stagnate there. We have to pick ourselves up and gather the strength to go on. Amma tells us that we should be like iron filings drawn towards a magnet. This intensity to merge with God should inspire us to stand up after every fall and keep going.

Someone recently told me that she was feeling sad and angry because she had been scolded for something she had not done. Even though she was not at fault, I advised her to just keep quiet and accept the scolding, even though the other party was clearly wrong and she was right. I knew the person she was in conflict with, and I felt that if she confronted him, there would be no end to the story. It was not the way she usually dealt with this kind of a problem, but she agreed to keep quiet. A few days later she told me that the person who chastised her had come back to apologise. The girl's quiet attitude showed him that he was wrong. He felt sorry for his poor behaviour and understood that he was the one who needed to change.

Sometimes we cannot help but blame others. This happens when we do not want to accept that we too are making mistakes. How quickly we would learn humility and accept our mistakes if we saw the people correcting us as Amma. If we could do that, how lovingly we would say to our critics, "I'm sorry, thank you for pointing out what I need to work on," even if it was not true!

When we maintain equanimity inside, no matter how crazy the outer situation, then the karmic bond that might have been born from our anger will be cut. If, on the other hand, we choose to fight, we may hold onto the conflict for years – possibly even into future generations.

We must learn to cut our karmic bonds, pull them out by their roots and totally dissolve our conflicts, otherwise we will find ourselves repeatedly acting out the same harmful scenarios. Situations and circumstances will continue to arise until we learn the lessons intended. We should aim to learn from our mistakes and attempt not to make them again. Each day we get the chance to start over. When someone points out that we have done something wrong, we should make an effort to accept as humbly as possible.

It is not helpful to think, 'I am a sinner. I have made so many mistakes. I will never learn. I cannot change myself.' How wrong this attitude is – we should always be ready to start again. Subtle blessings are always flowing towards us but we can only capture them by cultivating a positive attitude. We should not fall victim to hopelessness and failure.

There is no need to share your weaknesses with everyone as this will only serve to reinforce and strengthen them. When you make a mistake simply notice it and quietly accept; move forward trying not to repeat it. Strive to develop the humility to be happy if someone points out your shortcomings. It would be so beneficial if we could be grateful when we are corrected.

Making mistakes can be painful, but try to remember that this pain only comes to stop us from hurting ourselves. Every action we do will have repercussions that come along with it. We should not blame others, thinking, 'It is their fault, not mine.' When we take responsibility for our actions so many blessings start to emerge in life.

We are always ready to tell everyone when we have accomplished something great or done something extremely well. That is fine, but we also have to admit to ourselves that we do make mistakes sometimes. This can be very difficult, but do not worry, there will always be plenty of people around to point out our mistakes, faults and failures. Life offers endless chances to develop humility.

There is a story that I remember, when Amma severely chastised one of the swamis who had arranged for us to fly to Amma's Europe tour early on the morning of *Vijaya Dashami* (the festival celebrating victory over evil). This important festival in India marks a very auspicious time to initiate children into learning. Amma was upset because She wanted to be with everyone in the ashram at this time. Instead, the swami had arranged for one extra rest day in Germany after our arrival. Amma was not happy about it at all.

As we were leaving, She phoned the culprit from the car and scolded him saying, "Why did you do this? Why are you making me leave at this special time? I wanted to be with my children!" Where he was, on the other side of the world, it was three or four in the morning. The phone connection was terrible and he could not really understand what Amma was saying. It was clear that She was not happy with him, but instead of being upset, he thought about how sacred it was to hear the sound of Her voice at such an auspicious time of the morning. He became ecstatic because he knew that everything from Amma is a blessing, no matter what it is. Even a chastisement shows us that She really cares and wants to guide us to perfection. With joy in his heart at hearing Amma's words, he got off the phone, sat down and composed a bhajan.

It was such a wonderful way to accept his mistake. There he was being disciplined, but with the humble attitude of hearing the Guru's voice as a blessing, he turned the chastisement into divine music. We have a choice with everything that comes to us. Do we fight and let our ego rise up? Or do we surrender and turn the situation into a magnificent melody that we can share with the world?

We cannot control the situations or events that present themselves to us in life. The only thing that we can control is the attitude with which we accept them. Let us make an effort to turn everything into delightful bhajans that we can sing with Amma every night.

Chapter 13

Monster of the Mind

"The four hardest tasks on earth are neither physical nor intellectual feats, but spiritual ones: return love for hate; include the excluded; forgive without apology and be able to say, 'I was wrong.'"

– Author Unknown

We should strive to find peace of mind through all different types of trying situations. To maintain equanimity at all times is very difficult, but it is the true marker of blossoming spirituality. The waves of the mind are always trying to pull us down and drown us in the ocean of *maya* (illusion) that the world floats in. These mental waves can be stronger than a tsunami – they attempt to destroy everything. Our effort and spiritual practices will help us to maintain balance when it seems like we are walking on a tightrope, but they are not always enough to see us through complicated situations with the right attitude. This is why we need the guidance of a perfect Master.

There are yogis sitting in the Himalayas who have been meditating for decades but when it comes time to collect their meals, they may fight with each other over who gets to go first. They may be performing the most intense *tapas* (austerities), but sometimes very small things can quickly upset even the most experienced yogis. It is only through the profound grace of the Guru that the stubborn shadow of the ego can be gradually eliminated.

We must gain the grace that will allow our mind to hold onto peaceful awareness. This awareness is the greatest weapon that we can use to destroy the monsters that dwell within. It takes the grace and power of a perfect Master like Amma to fully conquer these monsters. Her love and guidance is guaranteed to eventually melt away all of our negativities and pain.

I often pray, 'Let my life be in service for Amma and may I gain the strength to be able to serve the world.' Inevitably as I am thinking this, my office doorbell rings, and I sigh to myself, 'Who is that disturbing me now?' I go out to see what the person wants. Usually it is someone coming to be helpful and I feel badly that I got annoyed. I go back to my seva and the doorbell rings again…sometimes as soon as I have sat down…and so the play goes on.

Then I remember and think to myself, 'What am I actually praying for? Here is a chance to fulfil my prayer and serve someone,' but I forget. Amma always reminds us that no matter how many years we have been in spiritual life – we are always beginners.

One can live near a Mahatma for decades, but unless our inner attitude is sincere and refined we will not grow or attain real peace of mind. One can be next to Amma for many years, but this will not guarantee anything unless we learn to use our mind properly. It is not enough to merely sit next to Amma, one must also put Her teachings into practice in our lives.

In the early days of the ashram, Amma had us sit in meditation for eight hours every day, which was tremendously difficult to do. She later admitted that one of the reasons She asked us to do this was because we always blamed external circumstances for our problems. It is so easy to fall into the trap of thinking, 'That person caused my troubles! It is everyone else's fault that I have problems!' When we sit down to practice meditation we see what is actually in our own mind. If we are honest, we will notice that we alone are the root cause of all our problems. Amma wants us to realise that we have to work on ourselves, instead of blaming others for the messy predicaments in our lives.

Being in Amma's presence and watching Her is truly a beautiful experience. I know that I am incredibly lucky to get the chance to be so close to Amma. When we are outside the ashram and travel in the camper over long distances, Amma may lie down on the floor to rest. Because of the extreme number of hours She spends sitting without a chance to stretch, Amma does not have very good circulation in Her legs, so I sometimes try to massage Her feet. This is one of the few little bits of comfort that She allows Herself in life, to very occasionally have Her feet massaged and even then She thinks of me first.

At times, if I am sitting on the floor and wanting to rub Her feet, Amma will stretch Her legs out towards me. She bends Her body into a totally uncomfortable position in order to make it practical and easy for me to reach Her. I feel so sad that in Her one moment of rest She is ready to make Herself uncomfortable, so that I can be comfortable.

The vibrations that come from Amma at this time are enough to calm the wild beasts in the mind. There have been times when I have found myself in tears thinking of how lucky I am to be physically close with Her. Amma's presence can create vibrations to make our mind melt and tame the vicious beasts that we keep caged inside, turning them into sweet little kittens. Sometimes when I touch Her feet I think of all the people who occasionally annoy me and I visualise going up to them and saying, 'I'm sorry. I forgive you.' All of my negativity melts away and I want to be good forever and surrender in all circumstances. In those moments, Her vibrations create so much love in me that the cast iron wall of the ego completely disintegrates.

The problem is that the wall only falls away temporarily. After some time, when I have stopped holding Her feet, it slowly gets built back up again and I think, 'Well, I don't *really* need to say anything to that person...'

Just one touch from Amma can make all of our negativities disappear into thin air. Regrettably, we usually allow them to come back again all too quickly. The ego persistently comes back to haunt us. Amma is able to break down the barriers inside of us, but it is up to us not to rebuild them. Luckily, Amma constantly forgives us and repeatedly encourages us to use our discrimination to do the right thing. It takes whole lifetimes of spiritual practices to retrain the negative flow of the mind and gain the strength and Divine grace that we need to reach the goal of seeing and experiencing Divinity everywhere.

We are here to learn how to master the mind, so that we can see the true beauty of creation, like Amma does. We must stop projecting blame onto others and be happy with what we are given. Every difficult problem that comes to us is actually a beautiful lesson in disguise. It is all designed by the Divine to teach us something that will help us to overcome our suffering. The problem is that we trust the enemy that is always trying to cheat us: our mind! We make this crazy mind our best friend and trust all of the absurd things it tells us.

Amma understands what we need to help us reach the state of equanimous vision, we should not doubt that, but it may not be easy to remember this truth when the dark clouds of maya obscure our discrimination. Amma has said that it can be so easy to see and feel the Divine but it is extremely difficult not to fall into the clutches of maya.

Say to yourself, 'Just let me be present in this moment and use my discrimination. Everything that comes to me is so that I can learn an important lesson.' Even though we may think that someone else or some external situation is the catalyst causing our problems, it is not true. All of our suffering comes only from the monsters in our own mind. Try to control those evil monsters before they swallow you up. If we try to make a conscious effort to control them, we will eventually gain the mental strength needed to permanently melt away all of our negativities.

It takes lifetimes of consciously trying to become good in order to reach the ultimate destination of God-realisation. Before we have to vacate this body, why not try our hardest to lead a virtuous life, little by little, however we can. The more we try, the easier it becomes. If we put in our best effort, then surely Amma's grace will eventually take us to the ultimate goal of God-realisation.

Chapter 14

Amma Melts Away All Negativities

> *"Renunciation means having the proper attitude. If you detach yourself mentally, you can keep the whole world around and it will never affect you."*
>
> *– Amma*

If we can keep our heads above water when the waves of existence threaten to drown us, then playing in the waves becomes a delightful experience. When we strive to see the joy in life and can remain grateful, especially through the most challenging times, life becomes a precious gift that will take us to the height of spirituality. In order to achieve this, we must strengthen our good qualities, which will help to reduce our

negative tendencies. Melting away all of our
selfishness is not an easy task.

The only way we can free ourselves from
mental pain and the demons that live inside of
us is to recognise them for what they really are.
Our true nature is pure love – but it is difficult,
almost impossible to love people when we feel
upset or totally annoyed at them. One girl I
know admitted to fantasising about scratching
people's eyeballs out when she is angry. So many
people in today's world have violent fantasies
whirling around inside their minds; even in
the Hindu scriptures it talks about a yogi who
became so angry, he turned a bird into a pile of
ash with just one glance.

It is important to cultivate internal detachment when these *vasanas* (negative tendencies)
arise inside of us. We should notice them and
try to change them, but we also must be careful
not to hate ourselves because of them. Telling
ourselves, 'I am so terrible because I have this
or that fault,' will only strengthen our attachment to the negativity. Try to notice the ways
you need to change, and strive to change them,

without becoming angry with yourself. Relax – everyone has faults – just do your best to scrub them clean.

We cannot always love everyone but at least we can try not to be angry with them when we feel upset. The only thing that blocks the pure essence of love inside of us from emerging is our anger and the ego. If we allow awareness to fill our mind, there will be no space at all for anger. Holding onto the awareness of the Divine in every moment will help our negativities to soften and dissolve. They can disappear in a flash when a positive thought arises to displace them.

A few years back, on tour in Mauritius, there was a teenage boy with us who was sometimes a bit mischievous. Someone ended up scolding him saying, "You are so naughty! You are so bad! You really shouldn't behave like this!" As I watched the situation unfold I imagined that the boy would get terribly upset at any moment but he just remained calm, detached and smiling. I was impressed by his self-control. It is extremely hard for teenagers to keep quiet and still (especially while being yelled at), but instead of getting angry and reacting, this boy kept quiet throughout the entire interaction.

Later on, I found out that the boy had discovered a Pizza Hut nearby. Before the chastisement, he had gone and bought some pizza and a soda and brought it back to the program. He was in such bliss to have something to eat other than Indian food. Even getting reprimanded could not shake him out of his happy mood. He was munching on his pizza and his only response to being scolded was to smile while replying, "You can say anything to me, it doesn't matter. Because I've got my pizza and I'm happy now!" I enjoyed this charming example of remaining totally in the present moment.

We should see our own lives in the same way. We have Amma, and because of this, we have everything. We have so much more than most people in the world. Here we are with the greatest Mahatma who has ever existed. We should try to see our lives like this boy saw his pizza. As 'cheesy' as it sounds, Amma is our 'deluxe pizza with everything!'

The truth is so simple, but very easy to forget – the mind will constantly try to cheat us. We should never become friends with the wavering mind, because like the flow of gravity, it is the nature of the mind to pull us downwards towards negativity. We can use the example of a pot full of crabs. If one crab tries to climb out and become free, the other crabs will quickly and tenaciously grab hold of it and pull it down. If the crabs at the bottom of the pot cannot free themselves, they will not allow any of the others to become free either. This classic example is known as 'crab syndrome.' If we are stuck in misery and restlessness, we only get a little peace of mind when we know that others are miserable as well.

In the West, a lot of mainstream psychology suggests going deep into our emotions and allowing ourselves to look at them and feel them as deeply as possible. Thoughts and emotions are fleeting and based in our ever-changing mind which is rooted in maya. They change constantly, so why do we give so much importance to them? To allow ourselves to indulge in them gives them more strength than they deserve, and only helps them to gain a greater hold over us.

I know a student who studied psychology for some time but felt that her mind was much more disturbed because of it. After one year of working with a therapist who encouraged her to delve deeply into her thoughts and emotions, her mind became so agitated that she had to take medicine in order to be able to sleep at night. Like ocean waves rolling towards the shore, our emotions are perpetually changing. Do not give them so much importance or they will drag you out to who-knows-where. Simply remain detached and watch from the shore as the waves flow in and out.

What I have found in my own life is that if I keep busy most of the time, focusing on getting my service work done, without letting my personal feelings get in the way, then I am totally taken care of. We tend to believe that we always have to think and feel and be in touch with our ever-changing, fleeting emotions. But when we think too much, it is easy to be carried away into a not so wonderful world filled with imaginary problems. We will be tossed around in a dark and turbid ocean of thoughts and then get repeatedly smashed against the rocks.

It is far better to try to channel our energy into something positive or to chant a mantra, than to get lost in illusory and deceptive thoughts.

It is said that God created everything in this world except the ego. That was man's creation, which is why it is so strong in us. We cannot overcome the ego on our own – we are too close to it and cannot see it clearly. Like a shadow, it follows us into all situations. The only guaranteed way to permanently dissolve it is through the grace of a perfect Master.

If we take Amma as our guide we are practically guaranteed that the trouble-making ego's days are numbered. Some people say you do not need a spiritual Master and that you can gain liberation on your own, but it is not really true. Only a very, very rare percentage of people are fit for a path without a Master. Most of us are not. The beauty of having a Guru is that She can separate us from our ego and take away all suffering and pain, replacing it with love.

Chapter 15

Selfless Service Leads to Grace

"It's all really very simple. You don't have to choose between being kind to yourself and others. It's one and the same."

— Piero Ferrucci

Amma reminds us that the sun does not need the light of a candle; likewise, God does not need anything from us because God is the giver of everything. We should realise that performing good actions and doing service are only for our own benefit. Grace flows to those who do selfless work and embody spiritual principles in their lives, even if they are not 'religious.' One of the greatest lessons that I have learnt from Amma is the power of selfless service to initiate a channel of Divine grace.

If someone comes and asks, 'Can you help me with this?' Help them. This is God coming in disguise, giving you an opportunity to open up your heart and melt away your selfishness. More often than not, the ways that we can help are quite simple. They do not take much time or effort, and who knows the grace that we can earn from doing this kind of thing. You will be more blessed by helping others than if you were to spend weeks in meditation. It is the small, self-less, simple jobs, nothing amazing, that entice grace towards us. Amma has told us time and time again that Her mind will keep remembering those who innocently offer their help, especially when they do not have to.

On the 2013 Europe tour, while travelling towards Holland, we were scheduled to stop in the late afternoon by a lake where Amma was going to serve everyone an early dinner. The menu had already been prepared: french fries and an Indian dish made of steamed rice balls with a sweet filling. As we waited for the staff buses to arrive the kitchen crew began preparing our evening meal. They set up stoves outside on the grass with big vats of hot cooking oil to fry the french fries. We waited more than an hour for the buses to arrive, but during that time the pleasant afternoon turned into a cold, dark and terribly windy evening. Amma decided that we should drive towards the Dutch program site instead.

As we drove out of the park I noticed that the cooking crew was still there with their pots of hot oil on the stove and numerous culinary ingredients all around. I felt so sorry for them and wondered how they would be able to safely transport the pans full of hot oil. Somehow they managed.

When we arrived at the hall Amma decided to feed everyone who had turned up there, which was well over 400 people. The cooking crew fried the potatoes and prepared a whole meal in record time. Amma served the meal, making everyone so happy. For many people at the program it was their first chance to be served by a spiritual Master (traditionally it is supposed to be the other way around, but Amma never follows this tradition. She is always the one who serves us). At the very end, just before Amma was about to stand up, She reached out and held the hand of the man who I had felt most sorry for, the head cook who had organised the tedious preparations. She took his hand and lovingly kissed it for no obvious reason at all. He was thrilled.

When we do not ask for anything in return, we are given more than we could ever hope for. Amma does not have to see us work, or even hear about it; Her grace flows spontaneously at just the right moment. It is one of the most beautiful lessons: when we give, we receive back so much more. If one merely takes throughout their life, what will they really be left with in the end? When we have experienced the value of giving, joy automatically fills our heart. We are rewarded a thousand times over.

When we stop thinking about ourselves and start focusing on others, we will find that the Divine provides us with everything that we need. We may not be given everything we want or desire, but when we see with the eyes of faith, we will realise that our needs are always taken care of. If something is missing, the Divine is simply teaching us a vaulable lesson.

Recently a devotee who does a lot of seva told a story about what happened when his bathing suit was disintegrating and he needed another one. Out of the blue, he was called by Amma's personal attendant and told that Amma had something for him. He was a little confused... what could Amma possibly have for him? He was handed a small package. He took the rubber-band off and looked inside. It was his old bathing suit that he had lost at the pool in Amritapuri two years before! A devotee from Mauritius had brought it to Amma and told Her that it was left behind at a program there (how his old bathing suit had travelled to Mauritius was an absolute mystery). Amma in turn was returning it to him...just in time. He appreciated then that She always provides us with everything that we need at exactly the right time.

Surrender to what presents itself and be happy with what you have. Remember that the Divine is always taking care of us. This is really the best rule to live by.

If it sometimes seems as though we are not receiving everything we need, or that despite our good actions, we are still suffering for no reason, we must remember that what we are experiencing now is the result of the actions we have performed in the past.

We have to be strong enough to face everything that comes to us in life, remembering that all hardships are a blessing in disguise. If we fight against everything, we will always suffer. We often end up thinking, 'No, this is wrong, it's a mistake. It's not right, it's not fair!' Try to remember that everything is for our *own* growth, to bring out the hidden talents that we have inside of us. If we can remember this, the journey of life will become far easier for us.

If we try to be good to people, that good will come back to us one day. We cannot do anything to change the past. Every action we have performed has a reaction, and that reaction is coming to us now. We cannot escape what is going to come to us, but what we do right now will determine our future. We cannot erase the past, but we can control our negative responses in the present by understanding the law of karma.

If we pray and strive to change our bad habits by doing good, then the grace of a Satguru can negate some of the negative karma due to come to us. She may not take everything away, because sometimes we have to suffer in order to learn something valuable; but when we sincerely extend the effort to be good, Amma can significantly reduce our suffering.

Everyone is always given exactly what they need by the Divine. When we do our spiritual practices properly and pray selflessly for others, then we will develop the mindset to remember this truth. That is the amazing thing about service: when we give to others we receive back so much more.

Chapter 16

The Divine Will Always Take Care of Us

"If we take care of today, God will take care of tomorrow."

— Mahatma Gandhi

Trust that the Divine knows how to take care of everyone. We are the only creatures in all of creation who endlessly worry about ourselves. When we believe that we will always be taken care of, we can focus our energy on helping others instead.

In the Bible, Jesus says, "Therefore I tell you, do not worry about your life, what you will eat or drink; or about your body, what you will wear. Is not life more than food, and the body more than clothes? Look at the birds of the air; they do not sow or reap or store away in barns, and yet your heavenly Father feeds them. Are you not much more valuable than they? Can any one of you by worrying add a single hour to your life? And why do you worry about clothes? See how the flowers of the field grow. They do not labour or spin. Yet I tell you that not even Solomon in all his splendour was dressed like one of these. If that is how God clothes the grass of the field, which is here today and tomorrow is thrown into the fire, will He not much more clothe you—you of little faith? So do not worry, saying, 'What shall we eat?' or 'What shall we drink?' or 'What shall we wear?'" (Matthew 6:25-32)

Several years ago, a very devotional man was informed that he was probably going to be laid off from his job. Since engineering jobs were difficult to find at that time, he knew that only grace could help him. Amma was on Her European tour, so he used the internet to find the city She was visiting and called the phone number listed under contact information. He knew that the chances were very slim that the busy host would actually answer the phone since

Amma was visiting their city. However, when he called, the host answered right away. He asked if he could speak to one particular Swami who just 'happened' to be standing right next to the phone. Swami took the call and told the devotee that he would inform Amma about him losing his job.

Five minutes after he made the call, his manager officially confirmed that he would lose his job. He immediately called Swami back again. Swami told him that as soon as he had entered Amma's room, before he could even tell Her what had happened, Amma remarked, "My engineer son just called you and is worried about his job situation." She continued, "He shouldn't worry; I will take care of everything."

He had complete trust that Amma would look after him and happily decided to spend his time off doing seva at the San Ramon ashram. While he was doing his service work, the wife of an engineer visited San Ramon and asked him if he knew of anyone who was looking for work. She was seeking to hire someone who had the exact skills he possessed.

We are given everything we need without asking. If we can try to learn to surrender with trust and faith to what is given, without demanding more, we will find that there is a stream of blessings flowing to us all of the time.

The Divine truly loves us and knows what is best for us, but we are like children who want only what we want and do not see the blessings in what we are given. One devotee, who is a teacher, tells a story about one of her students:

> "There was a young man in my class this past year. He played football, was handsome, charming and friendly with his other classmates. He was very bright, but terribly undisciplined. Each day he would come into the classroom happy and playful but when it was time to get to work he would begin to whine and complain bitterly.
>
> "Miss, I hate this class, it's too much work, I'm going to fail, I'm not even going to try, I can't do it anyway, you make it too hard." Every day the same story.

I would be gentle, I would be tough, I would be compassionate, I would be stern, but always I would say, "Yes you can, and yes you will."

Now I must admit, I became over-whelmed by all of his complaining… month after month the battle would continue. His grade would slip and he couldn't play football if it was below a C, so he came after school and I helped him catch up in the afternoon, but the next morning the same old complaints came back again.

In frustration I finally started separating him from his friends and had him sit in another room so he could concentrate. He became even more angry and hostile, but every day I would send him to his new spot. Then finally one day, when neither one of us expected it, Amma showed up in her undercover way.

The boy started goofing off and I said, "OK, time to go in the office by your-self." He began to whine and complain and I continued, "Do you know what the *real* problem is here?" I was serious and he knew it.

He asked, "No, what is the real problem?"

I said, "Sweetheart, the real problem is that you think I am punishing you, but I'm not. The real problem is that you just don't know that *this is what love looks like*." He stopped cold in the middle of the room...you could hear a pin drop. I could see the little wheels turning in his head.

He looked at me with such surprise, "Really Miss?"

I replied, "Yes dear, this is love, now get to work."

He settled down away from his friends and worked steadily for the rest of the hour. At the end I came up behind him and put my hand on his head and said, "See, you do such good work once you start. You just need some help getting started."

Now I would like to say that he never whined again but that wouldn't be true.

He still caused trouble sometimes, but from that day on I could just catch his eye, say his name, and I could see him remembering the words, 'This is what love looks like,' and he would settle in again.

The unexpected blessing for me is that now, whenever I find myself whining about what the Divine has brought into my life, I feel as though I can hear Amma's voice telling me, 'Do you know what the real problem is? The real problem is that you just don't know that *this is what love looks like!*'

This truth might be hard to remember sometimes, especially when times are difficult – but if we can surrender to the Divine will, and find the love in it, then our lives will surely be blessed. Sometimes the outside world seems like a fight, but Amma reminds us that the real battlefield is within ourselves. It is the negative emotions such as fear, anger, jealousy and lack of faith that are our true enemies.

Amma is like Sri Krishna driving the chariot for us through our struggle. She patiently waits for us to turn to Her for guidance. We should cultivate the habit of praying and talking to the Divine, developing an inner conversation with our true Self, rather than listening to the negative thoughts chattering away trying to misguide us. When we remain centred, instead of getting carried away by our thoughts and emotions, the mind will become more clear and controlled. We will find all of the answers we need; they are patiently waiting inside of us, ready to bubble forth when we give them a chance.

Chapter 17

Finding Our True Dharma

"There is a wonderful mythical law of nature which states that the three things we crave most in life - happiness, freedom and peace of mind - are always attained by giving them to someone else."

– Peyton Conway March

Our true dharma in life is to know who we are and to serve others. We all want a good future – this is made from what we do in the present. The present is all that we have, so just do good things now. It is that simple. Why do we tend to complicate everything so much?

Living an honourable life and performing kind actions whenever we can is the reason we are here. It is far more important to live and act in a dharmic way than it is to try and make sense of our ever-changing thoughts and emotions. Too much of our energy is focused on the fluctuating world of what we think and feel. Simply remember that you are always taken care of and do not waste time worrying (so little of what we worry about actually happens); instead of focusing on yourself, use your energy to focus on others. If we strive to live up to these highest ideals, we will find peace.

I remember one day while we were travelling in America, Amma asked a young child who was in the vehicle with us, "What is the reason you were you born?"

He replied, "Uhh, I don't know."

Amma answered the question for him. "To know who you are and to help others. Say this five times."

So he repeated it, "To know who I am and to help others. To know who I am and to help others. To know who I am and to help others. To know who I am and to help others. To know who I am and to help others."

"Don't ever forget that," She told him seriously. She said he should say it to himself five times every day so he would always remember.

This is dharma in life: to know who we are and to help others.

We usually want to know everyone else's business, but we rarely look into who *we* are. We are always turning outside for answers, never turning inside; yet, that internal inquiry is what the journey of our existence is all about. We are here to understand who we really are and why we are here.

While sitting in front of Amma we might enjoy Her attention for a while, but this is not enough. To fully experience inner peace, we must earn the grace to control our own mind. This is the ultimate task to master, but also the most difficult.

Amma might smile at us or shower love upon us for some time, leading to temporary bliss, but this is not the ultimate goal. The goal is to become established in that bliss all the time, which requires going deeply within to the source of our being. Many young people today are looking to 'find themselves,' but even with this goal in mind, most end up travelling in the wrong direction. It takes an extremely strong and courageous spirit to journey on the path towards the real goal, that of finding our true Self, the eternal Self, which is one with the Divine.

I remember one day I was sitting in a leadership workshop. Many people had turned up who wanted to be leaders. Everyone seemed very excited, they were eager to find out what the secret was. He spoke on and on.

Frankly, I must admit, I found it quite boring. There was not anything that really attracted me in what was being said, until we got near the very end and there was one line that this man said, "Find out what your gift is in life, what you're good at, and use that to serve others." When I heard that, I thought this whole class had been worth sitting there just to hear that statement.

It really stuck in my mind, this is what the dharmic role is for us in life. To find out what our gifts are in life and to use them to serve. That is what many great leaders have done in this world. It is what Amma's life has been. When She was young, She found out She had a gift to comfort people. She has used Her life to do exactly this, totally following Her dharmic path.

Countless people ask Amma, "Amma, what is my dharma? What sort of seva/school/job should I be doing?" The most important thing is not *what* we do, but rather *how* we do it. Our attitude behind the action is what matters. The work we do should not define who we are. The crucial thing is simply to serve others, in whatever ways we can, using our talents to the best of our ability.

It is easy to earn the grace of the Divine, but to become a genuinely good person is much more difficult. To always do the right thing, perform only selfless actions and always think well of others – to train the wild beast that lives in our mind – is a monumental task. This should not scare us; we do not need to be slaves, always sacrificing ourselves for others. It is okay to make sure that our needs are taken care of first. After all, it takes an incredible amount of unrelenting effort to become an authentic human being. The struggle to find the genuine 'humane' inside of us is a lifelong quest. One needs a heroic spirit to accomplish this feat.

One devotee tells this story: "Growing up both of my parents were alcoholics. Violence, drugs and alcohol were the only thing I knew. I started drinking in my early teens and started doing drugs shortly afterwards. Soon I was drinking and smoking every night. I continued this habit for nearly twenty years. I was completely lost and consumed in my addictions. I tried to stop on several occasions, but was never strong enough. I was consumed by selfishness and self-loathing. I only felt peaceful when I was high.

When I came to Amma, my whole life transformed. I felt an instant connection with Her and was overwhelmed by Her love. I immediately knew that She wanted more from me than to stay lost in the drugs and alcohol. I stopped both addictions the night that I received my first darshan – I have been clean ever since.

Watching Amma give darshan I am so inspired by the love and affection that She showers on everybody. She has inspired me to stop my destructive habits and spend my time helping others instead. Instead of drinking, I now spend my evenings volunteering. Amma has guided me onto the path towards true love and inner peace."

It is extremely rare to find inspiring role models. Hardly anyone lives with the highest intentions and noblest values incorporated into their lives. The values of peace, love and compassion cannot just be words on a page; we must strive to express them in our actions. It is not enough to think that we will do great things in the future. It is the present *now* that we need to work on. We should not keep wasting our lives away, planning to change in the future. We dream up so many apologies for not acting better now. Let go of the 'but/ if only/when this all changes' excuses. Amma reminds us that this life is not a dress rehearsal. This is it…here and now.

Challenge yourself to perform according to the highest ideals (you know you should!), otherwise life will burn away in vain. Our energy is burnt up so quickly in unproductive pursuits; instead, strive to serve in whatever ways you can. If we can hold onto this sacred intention, we will earn the grace of our own mind and find within us the true peace that we all long for.

Having compassion is not as difficult as we may think. It is our birthright and our saving grace. When Amma gives free education to children through Her scholarship programs, She has one stipulation: after they have finished their education, and are settled in life, they should pay it back by sponsoring another child who does not have the money to continue their education. In this way, Amma creates a beautiful butterfly effect where the good things in life are passed on and on. We have received so many blessings in our lives; let us express our gratitude through service.

Amma's message for us is theoretically very simple: strive to love everyone and to serve others in whatever small way you can. Amma does this in Her every action, with Her every breath. With a little bit of effort, combined with Amma's guidance and grace, we too will find Her tremendous love available inside of ourselves.

Chapter 18

Have a Little Faith

*"You are not a drop in the ocean. You
are the entire ocean in a drop."*

— *Rumi*

When surveys have been conducted to find
out who is happier, people who believe in a
higher power, or those without any faith at all,
it is always shown that people with faith enjoy
greater happiness in their lives.

No one can force us to have faith. It is
something we have to develop ourselves. If we
have faith, true faith in God or Guru, that faith
cannot be shaken by anyone or anything. True
faith is immovable and unchangeable. We have
to listen to our own heart, mind and intellect
to develop faith – there is no force involved, it
simply dawns in us when we are walking on the
path towards love.

Sometimes people think, 'Oh, I am not going to blindly believe that Amma is my Guru, so I am going to ask Her.' They come up to Amma during darshan and say, "Amma, are you my Guru?" Amma is so humble and compassionate, these qualities naturally flow from Her. So when we ask Her if She is our Guru, it is never a problem. She never minds. She is always ready to come down so low, to our level, and lovingly say, "Yes, yes child, I am your Guru."

Amma is the greatest spiritual Master that has ever existed. If we use our awareness and discernment, this truth becomes evident. Look, see and feel Her power; even the vibrations that come from Amma are powerful enough to show us who She really is. Consider the way She has lived Her life. She absolutely can take us from darkness to light, but our cooperation and awareness must be there as well.

Some people can automatically feel the Divine presence of great souls, as they have a spiritual foundation to understand these things. They can easily fine-tune themselves to tap into the vibration emanating from an enlightened Master. Yet, many more may not have reached that level and just view Amma as a sweet woman who gives great hugs and runs an amazing charity network. Ultimately, what people think or say about Her makes no difference to Amma at all. She simply flows to the world as a mighty river of love, leading us back to that same source if we care to follow. What we choose to do with Her life-giving water is entirely up to us – the river simply flows.

A Satguru sees the past, present, and future. When Amma looks at us, She knows everything in all of these different realms. She has the power to tune into other dimensions if the need arises. This does not mean that She judges us with Her knowledge. She is always understanding and compassionate.

When we look at Amma we cannot remember the past, tell the future or even dwell in the present for more than a few seconds. We look at Her and due to our limited capabilities we wonder, 'Does She really know me? Does She completely understand what is going on?' She does. Have no doubt about that. So many have been blessed with the direct experience of Amma's omniscience.

When Amma's brother was a teenager he had never tried smoking or drinking. One day, while he was hanging out with another teenager who lived nearby, this friend tempted him to try a cigarette. Amma's brother did not know what to do. He felt it was wrong to smoke and did not want Amma to find out that he was tempted by it, but he also felt a little excited by the idea. His friend suggested, "Let's meet here tomorrow and I'll bring a cigarette for you to try."

The next morning, when Amma's brother was milking the cows, Amma approached him, "Do you smoke?" She asked. He froze and did not reply. She continued, "I know that you don't...so DON'T!" He was shocked by the warning in Her voice. Even though he had not yet tried smoking, he was planning on trying it later that day. He realised that Amma had found him that morning in order to keep him from going astray. Afterwards, he was always careful not to behave badly or go in the wrong direction.

Most of Amma's relatives do not get as much of a chance to spend time with Her as they did while they were growing up. It may be a long time before Amma calls to speak with them and

sometimes they feel sad about this. This same brother sometimes thinks, 'I'm not doing anything bad, that's why Amma doesn't call me. If I did something wrong, then Amma would call.' Whenever he desires to do something that he knows Amma would not approve of, his policy is always to tell Amma mentally first and then to tell his wife.

One day he became so frustrated that Amma was not calling him that he decided to finally try smoking. As per his policy, he told Amma first, mentally, and then openly told his plan to his wife. She was surprised, but said nothing. The very next moment, the phone rang. He asked his wife to answer it. She refused, so he took the phone himself. It was Amma on the line, calling him to come to Her room to see Her. Even though it was just an idle threat that he would go off and smoke, Amma called him immediately.

This does not mean that we should threaten to perform bad actions for the sake of Amma's attentions, but it does show just how much She understands and cares about us. Amma is always praying that we engage in the correct behaviour.

Her sole desire is that we walk in the dharmic direction on the path towards love.

There is no better offer anywhere in this world than to take refuge at Her lotus feet. Feel free to go out and look, but you will not find a better Guru anywhere in this creation. Amma is the silent witness to everything, constantly giving grace, bliss and love. She offers so much more than we can possibly understand.

The mother that gave birth to us will look after us for a few years, but Amma promises to come back until the end of time in order to take us to the ultimate goal of liberation from our suffering. She is not going to force us; She will simply hold our hand and guide us along the way. Sometimes, if it is in our best interest, She might push us forward a little when we start to hesitate. She might make us face things that we do not really want to face, but the power of Her love is so strong that it can help us to overcome any challenge that might arise.

People have been wounded by so many experiences in life. Love has more of a healing effect than anything in this world. This is what Amma is offering.

Amma is the manifestation of our own true Self. She is already full and complete. She does not desire anything from anybody, including love or devotion. The truth is that it is we who need Her. We are the ones who benefit from our faith in Amma. Her love and guidance will only bring joy to our lives.

Every single devotee has amazing stories of their experiences with Amma, but we forget them so quickly. We listen to the fickle mind and to fickle people. We think, 'No, maybe Amma's not enlightened: She is playing favourites; She isn't looking at me at all; She is talking to that person all the time!' Or some other silly reason. Amma will not be pulled into the dramas that we play, even though it may seem like that at times. She may react to different situations, expressing various emotions such as sadness or anger; but inside She remains unmoved.

Amma is completely established in the ultimate understanding; She is always experiencing the Divine inherent in every atom of this creation. Liberation is an exalted state of mind. That is why it is said that we should never judge a Master – their mind works in a different way than ours. When we allow ourselves to stop and objectively observe Amma the truth becomes obvious: Amma is simply an embodiment of pure love.

There is no escape from love. Sooner or later, we all must surrender to this truth and become embodiments of love as well. Amma is a messenger of love, the manifestation of pure power and selflessness and She is here to bring us from darkness, to light. She has come to remind us of who we really are.

The greatest thing I have learned from Amma is that the power of love really is the answer to everything.